free pick

P9-CAN-532

Sweet as a Rose

An I WONDER WHY Reader

HOLT, RINEHART AND WINSTON, INC.

New York   Toronto   London   Sydney

Sweet as a Rose

by Lawrence F. Lowery and Albert B. Carr

Consultant, ABRAHAM S. FISCHLER
Illustrated by JUNE GOLDSBOROUGH

Library of Congress Catalog Card Number: 69-20255
SBN:-03-081170-8

90123 52 987654321

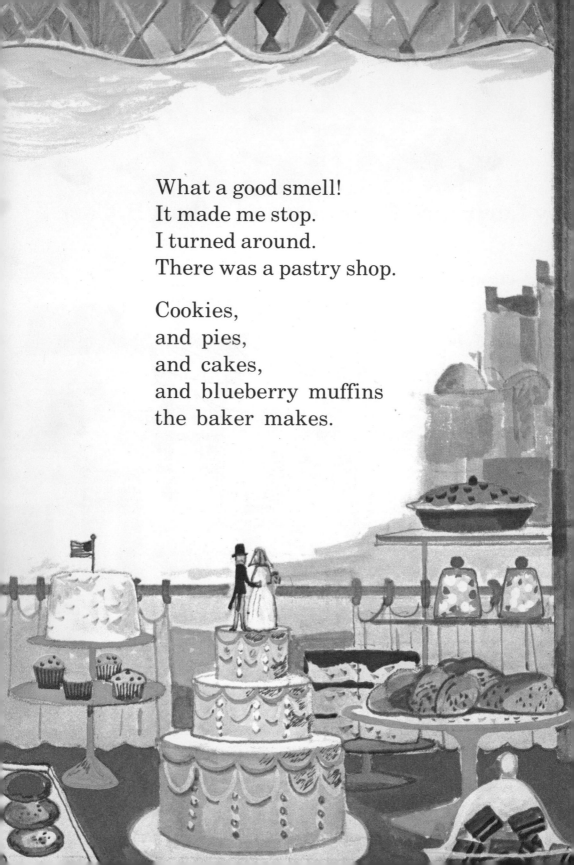

What a good smell!
It made me stop.
I turned around.
There was a pastry shop.

Cookies,
and pies,
and cakes,
and blueberry muffins
the baker makes.

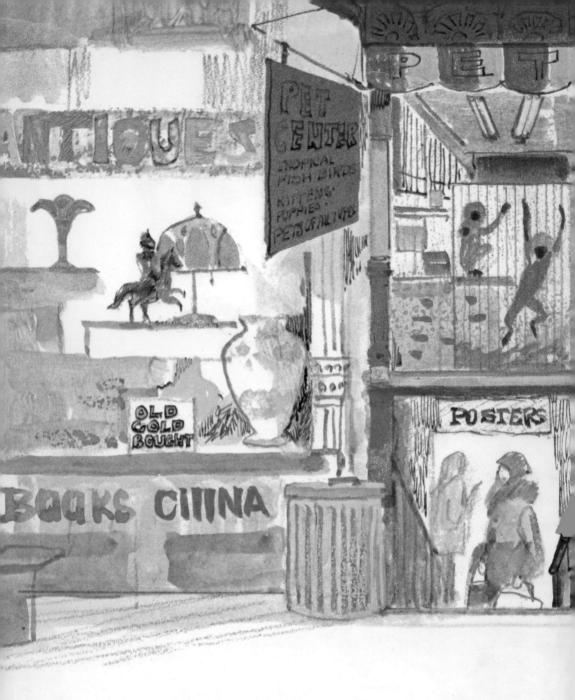

What an odd smell!
I came to a stop.
Do you know what I saw?
A red and yellow pet shop.

There were birds and monkeys,
and kittens and cats,
and three brown puppies
at play on their mats.

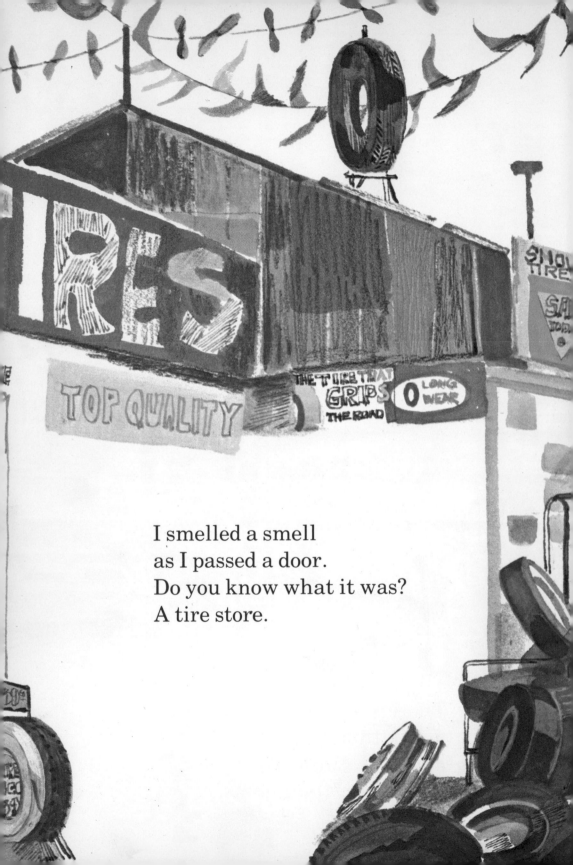

I smelled a smell
as I passed a door.
Do you know what it was?
A tire store.

Rubber tires
for big cars and small!
Rubber tires
for trucks that are tall!

What is that smell?
I'll have to think hard.
I know! Across the street
is a lumber yard.

Pine wood,
and oak,
and maple, too.
There are walnut and cedar,
and the smell of wood glue.

I smelled a bad smell
and wrinkled my nose.
Could it be that cart
of wrinkled old clothes?

Scraps,
rags,
and dirty bags.
Rubbish in a clump,
all ready for the dump.

There was a smell
as strange as any I had found.
Men were digging
a big hole in the ground.

Dust
and dirt were
blowing in my face.
Men with shovels were all over the place.

I smelled a smell
that was not very sweet.
It was tar being poured
on top of our street.

That tar was thick and
black and hot.
The best thing to cover a
a street's bad spots.

I smelled a smell
from where I stood.
From a shoemaker's shop
came a smell that was good.

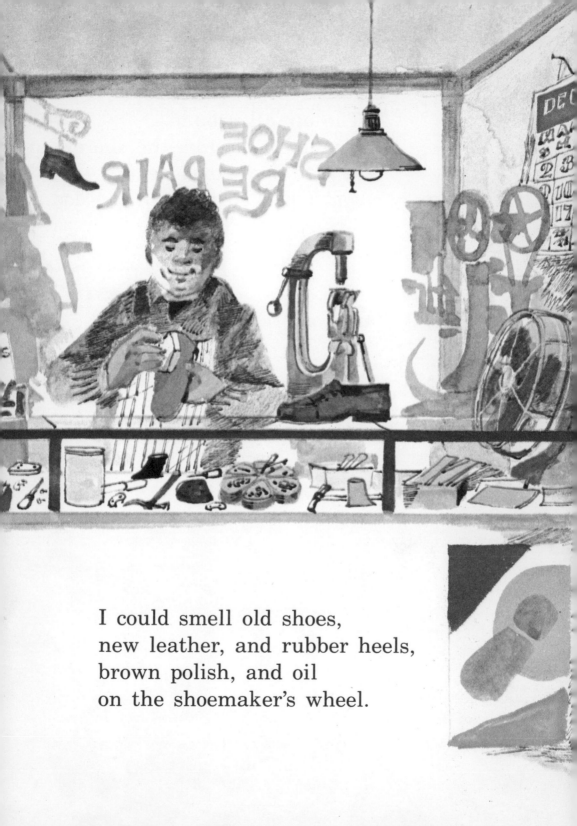

I could smell old shoes,
new leather, and rubber heels,
brown polish, and oil
on the shoemaker's wheel.

The air all around
smelled a bit like the shore.
A fish shop stood near,
and I peeked through the door.

There were cod fish and sunfish,
and fresh lobsters' tails,
bluefish, butterfish,
and glass jars of snails.

A sweet country smell
was on every side.
It came from a fruit shop
with its door opened wide.

I saw apples and oranges,
bananas and berries,
peaches and melons,
plums, pears, and cherries.

The smell was as sweet
as a fairyland.
It came through the air
from a flower stand.

I saw violets and daisies,
lilies and roses,
sunflowers, tulips,
and all kinds of posies.

There was a smell
as I neared home.
It was the smell of clean laundry
swish swashing in foam.

The smell of bleach,
soapsuds and cloth,
jingling, tumbling,
in bright white froth.

On the first day of spring
I smelled a new thing.
Everywhere I would pass
was the sweet smell of grass.

A fresh wind was blowing.
The green grass was glowing.
All through the park
new plants were growing.

Everywhere I go
there is a new smell to know.

Is there a place with no smell?
Who can tell?